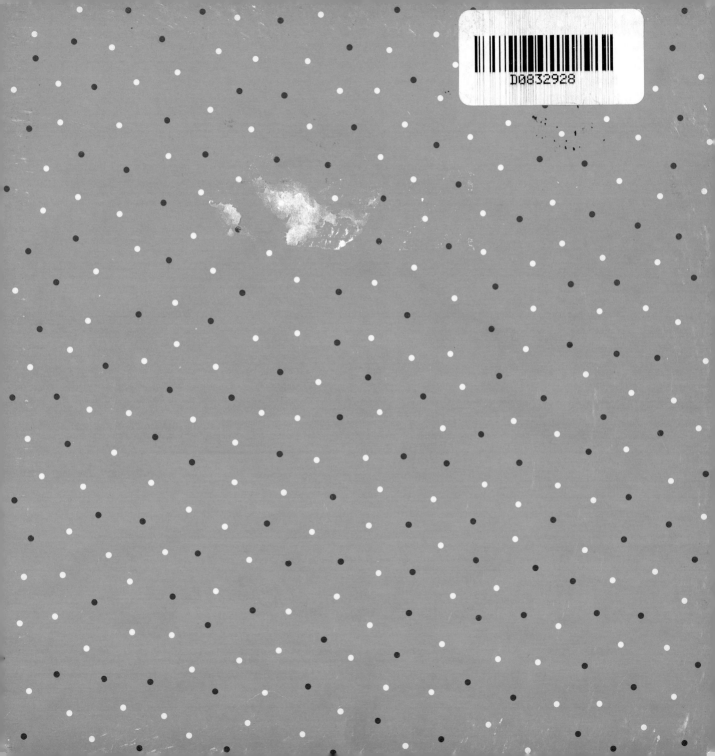

A DORLING KINDERSLEY BOOK

Note to Parents

My First Look At Nature is designed to help young children learn
about the plants and animals they see in the natural world - in ponds and rivers,
by the seashore, or in the garden. It's a book for you and your child to share
and enjoy – looking at the pages together, finding familiar animals
and objects, and learning and using new words.

Editors Andrea Pinnington,
Charlotte Davies
Designer Heather Blackham
Managing Editor Jane Yorke
Senior Art Editor Mark Richards
Series Consultant Neil Morris
Photography Steve Gorton

Additional Photography Peter Chadwick,
Philip Dowell, Paul Goff, Frank Greenaway,
Colin Keates, Dave King, Stephen Oliver,
Kim Taylor, and Jerry Young
Animals supplied by Trevor Smith's
Animal World, Intellectual Animals,
and the Natural History Museum, London

First published in Great Britain in 1991
by Dorling Kindersley Limited,
9 Henrietta Street, London WC2E 8PS
Reprinted 1993

A CIP catalogue record for this book is available from the British Library.

ISBN 0-86318-607-6

Reproduced by Bright Arts, Hong Kong
Printed and bound in Italy by L.E.G.O.

·MY · FIRST · LOOK · AT ·

Nature

DK

DORLING KINDERSLEY
London • New York • Stuttgart

Flowers

Flowers grow from seeds and bulbs.

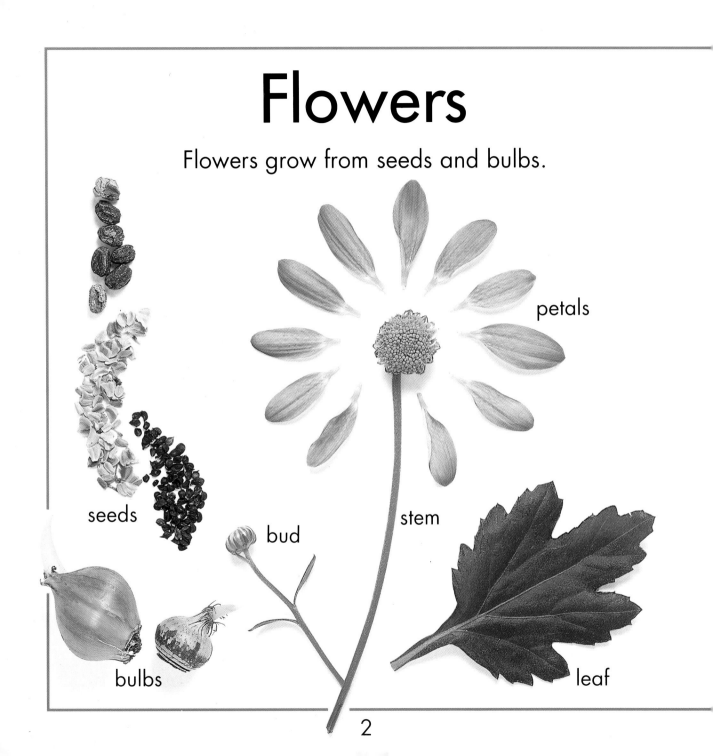

petals

seeds

bud

stem

bulbs

leaf

rose

freesia

carnation

tulip

lily

delphinium

Minibeasts

You can find these minibeasts in the garden.

honeycomb

honey
bee

bumble bee

snail

centipede

spider

ladybirds

worms

grasshopper

Caterpillars turn into butterflies.

caterpillar

chrysalis

butterfly

5

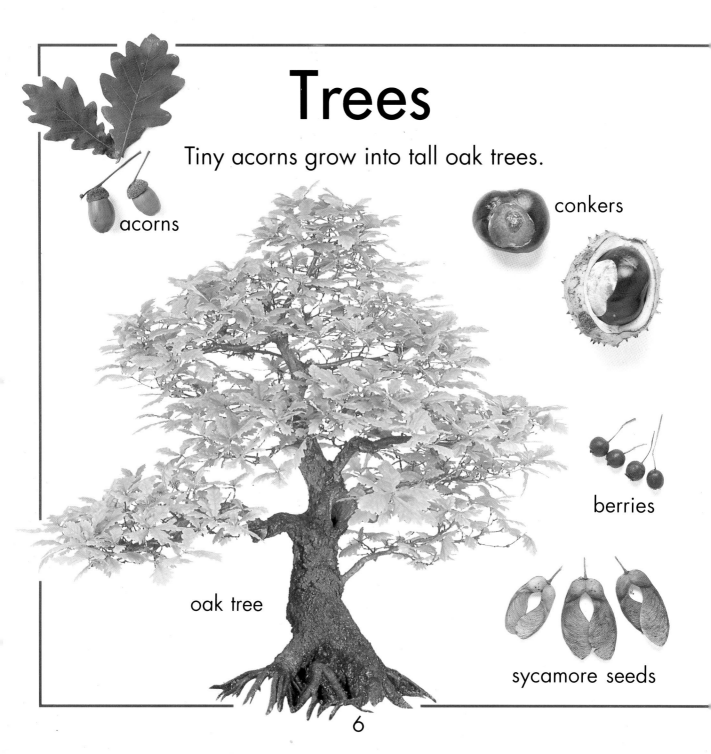

Trees

Tiny acorns grow into tall oak trees.

acorns

conkers

berries

oak tree

sycamore seeds

6

leaves

bark

cone

branch

conifer

7

Animals

Have you seen any of these animals in the countryside?

lizard

bat

squirrel

mouse

snake

rabbit

Birds

Most birds lay their eggs in nests.

owl

bird's
nest

birds' eggs

feathers

pheasant

sparrow

11

By the river

Many plants and animals live in rivers, ponds, and lakes.

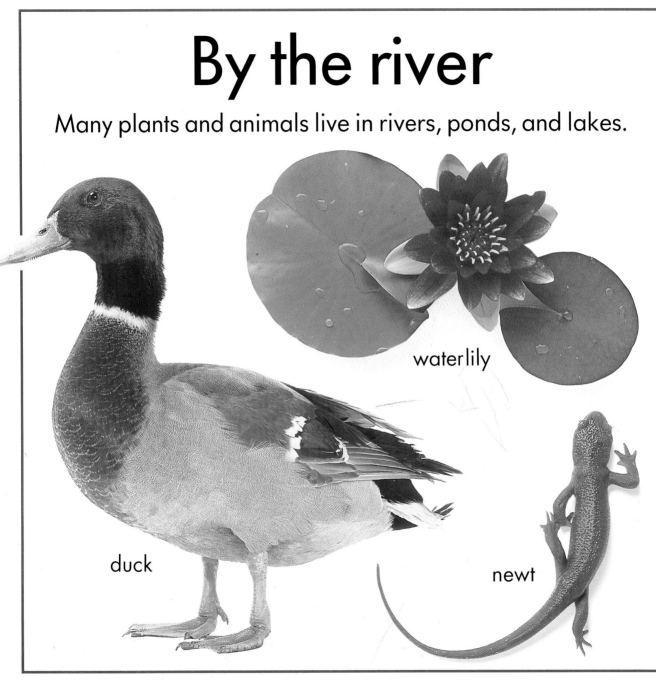

water lily

duck

newt

fish

frog
spawn

tadpole   dragonfly

frog

Tadpoles turn into frogs.

bulrushes

At the seaside

How many of these things have you
seen on the beach?

seahorse

sea urchins

crab

sand

seaweed

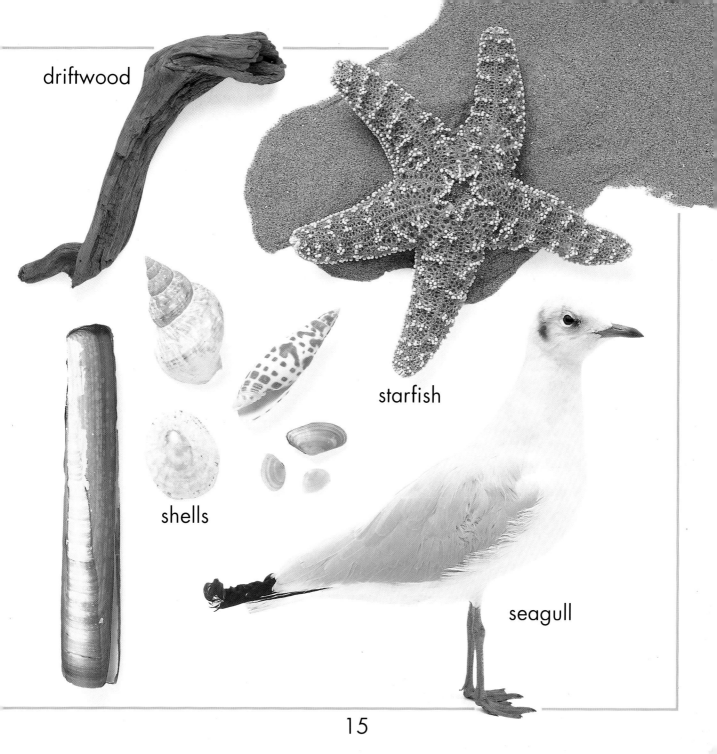

driftwood

starfish

shells

seagull

15

Can you remember?

What do these things grow into?

acorns

egg

frog spawn

bulbs

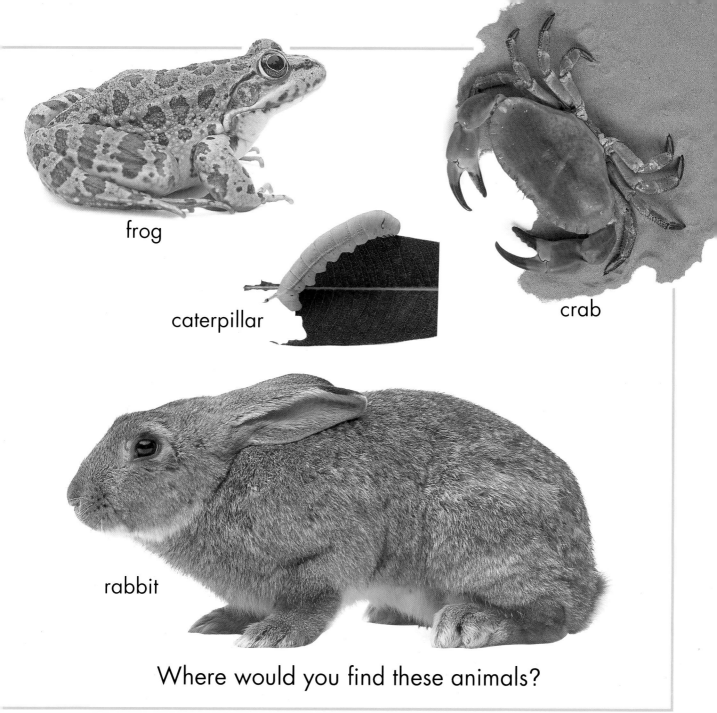

frog

caterpillar

crab

rabbit

Where would you find these animals?

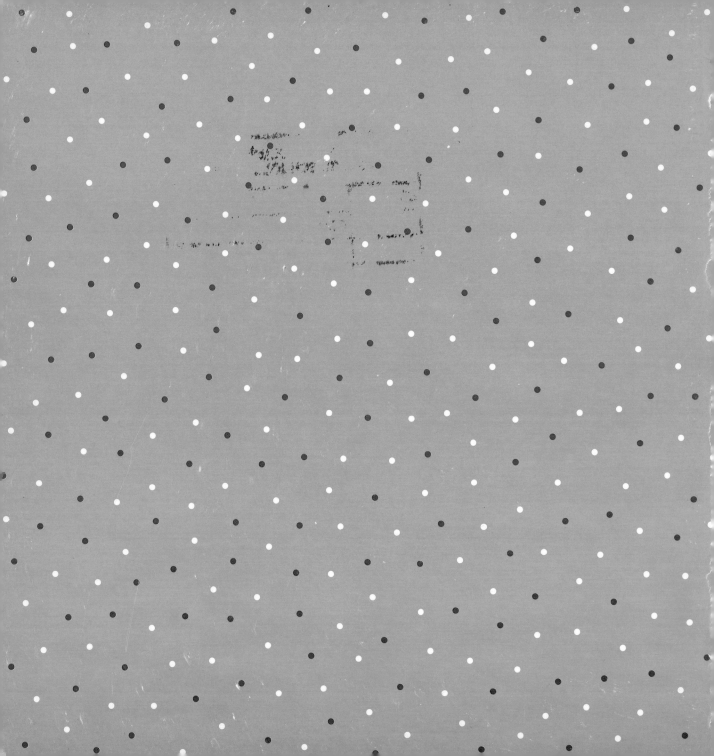